A CANADIAN BRASS CHRIS

T0082001

arranged for brass quintet with optional keyboard
by
Luther Henderson

Conductor's Score

Note: All arrangements in this collection may be played by either quintet alone, or quintet with keyboard/synthesizer accompaniment.

each part is published separately:

Trumpet I in B flat
Trumpet II in B flat
Horn in F
Trombone
Tuba
Keyboard/Synthesizer
Conductor's score

Recorded on the CBS release "A Canadian Brass Christmas" (FMT-39740).

Bring a Torch, Jeannette, Isabella

traditional French carol
arranged by Luther Henderson

Piu lento

Ding Dong! Merrily On High

traditional carol
arranged by Luther Henderson

*Play notes in parentheses in absence of chimes, in buckets or into stands.

Go Tell It On The Mountain

19th century Negro Spiritual
arranged by Luther Henderson

God Rest Ye Merry Gentlemen

Note: This piece can be played with, or without the Synthesizer-Keyboard part.

London carol, 19th century tune
arranged by Luther Henderson

Here We Come A-Wassailing

traditional carol from the north of England
arranged by Luther Henderson

The Huron Carol

traditional carol
arranged by Luther Henderson

I Saw Three Ships

traditional English carol
arranged by Luther Henderson

Sussex Carol

traditional English carol
arranged by Luther Henderson

B
Tpt. 1.
Tpt. 2
Fr. Hn.
Trb.
Tuba
Synth.
Kbd.
leg.
mf
mp
mp
mp
mp
mp
30
Tpt. 1
Tpt. 2
Fr. Hn.
Trb.
Tuba
Synth.
Kbd.